ISLE OF VIEW
INSIGHTS

INSPIRATIONAL ACRONYMS & ART
TO TRANSFORM YOUR WORLD

by

RUSSELL McDOUGAL

Isle of View
3211 Walnut Street
Boulder, Colorado 80301
303-444-MYTH
Toll free 1-866-344-VIEW (8439)
www.isleofview.biz

ISBN 0-9754066-1-2

Printed in China

"I love the Isle of View cards. They stretch the mind and stretch the heart."

- *Marianne Williamson*

"At once whimsical and profound, McDougal's Insight Cards are a delight".

- *Judith Simmer-Brown, Chair - Religious Studies at Naropa University*

"McDougal's magical "Isle of View Insight Cards" are a refreshing source of illumination for today's troubled times. These cards… are the mystical antidote to those 'end time blues'. Yes, magic is still alive, and picking one of Russ's cards any time during your day is a sure way of reminding yourself of this fact…Oh yes, 'Magic', in McDougal's syntax is 'Mind's Awareness Generates Infinite Creation'. That's Russ himself!"

- *Jose Arguelles, author, co-founder Earth Day & Harmonic Convergence, planetary whole systems anthropologist, Mayan Scholar*

"How we see the world determines what we do in the world. These cards will inspire new eyes."

- *Mark Victor Hansen, Co-creator, #1 New York Times best selling series Chicken Soup for the Soul; Co-author, The One Minute Millionaire*

"The meaning of life is to give life meaning."
-Author unknown

"There's more to life than having everything."
-Maurice Sendak

"We shall not cease from exploration, and the end of all of our exploring will be to arrive where we started and know it for the first time."
-T.S. Eliot

"Things don't change. You change your way of looking, that's all."
-Carlos Castaneda

"The world only exists in your eyes – your conception of it. You can make it as big or as small as you want to."
-F. Scott Fitzgerald

"There's still time, but there ain't forever."
-Rick Sylvester

"Shoot for the moon. Even if you miss, you'll land among the stars."
-Les Brown

Dedication

I dedicate this work to all beings,
especially Mother Earth, the plants and animals,
and most especially my parents
Dr. Burton and Louise McDougal,
my sons, Austin and Connor,
and my siblings Nona Jane,
Louann and Dan.

Isle of View Insights

Come to the Isle of View and discover your mind's island paradise is waiting for you. Come to the Isle of View and learn to say, "I love you." Find ageless wisdom distilled to a word-phrase insight that reflects and reawakens the sparkle of your life. These insights offer a unique way to awaken the magic and joy of being alive. The acronyms show you how to "know how now". They are food for thought, simply wonderful hors d'oeuvres on the meaning of life. They can function as keys to unlock some of life's most important lessons. They are magical transformative messages that can open you up to the inherent wonder of your life. The fun and wisdom of this knowledge are yours for the tak- ing. Isle of View is a magical vision of poise and balance in an ocean of change. Isle of View opens you to that knowing place of openness and contentment. These visions works at each moment and at every level. They are inspirational to school children and practiced travelers alike. This knowledge offers a wonderfully unique way of seeing and interpreting your world. When you see your world in a new way, the world literally changes for you.

The intention is to share a transformative vision that gives people the insight and inspiration to find the magic in their lives right now. Russell says, "Remember, we're all in this gift of life together and all One in this grand, living mosaic of life. It is life. L.I.F.E. - Let It Flow Effortlessly.

When you can see really clear, you can let go of fear, and realize that your paradise is already here.

Your Mind Is The Cake
by Russell McDougal

When you finally are amazed
And never are bored
You can ride the magic ship
that we're all aboard.

When you finally realize
you have what it takes
You can finally give worry
its final shakes.

When you finally realize
you have the recipe to bake
You can finally realize
that your mind is the cake.

When you finally realize
There's no more than you have
You can know that the mind
is its own healing salve.

When you finally realize
that there's nothing to know
You can find contentment
with no need to go.

When you finally realize
that its all in the mind
You can mirror the magic
and leave doubt behind.

About the Artist

Russell McDougal has been an artist, photographer, and poet for over 30 years. The philosophy of awareness and authentic seeing lie at the core of his art. These visions come from discovering the extraordinary in the ordinary, everyday experience seen through the eyes of an artist.

At the beginning of his career, Russell produced **Mirror of Mind**, a book of his photographs, coupled with quotations from wise sources throughout the worlds of religion, philosophy, music and psychology. The book was his first attempt at combining words and visual images in a simple format that most anyone could understand. The **Isle of View Insights** and other **Isle of View** productions carry on this work of re-minding people of their inner wisdom. Russell traveled extensively and studied philosophy for many years. He lives in Boulder, Colorado after 10 years in San Francisco. He has two wonderful sons, Austin and Connor. He has a photo/design studio housing a vast, world-class collection of art objects and archives of vintage art, as well as his collection of photographs.

Acceptance Brings Contentment

Each instant is perfectly "as it is", no more and no less. If we can accept it, we can find peace. If we want it to be different than it is, we create our own unhappiness. Do you really think that any instant can ever be different than it is? This moment is exactly "as it is". Accept it and find contentment and peace of mind. So much suffering in our world is simply caused by wanting things to be different than they are. It's totally fine to try to create change, but for now this is how it is. Highest knowledge is to simply acknowledge that each moment is just what it is. It's as simple as ABC.

A B C
ACCEPTANCE BRINGS CONTENTMENT

© R. McDougal, 2004

Arrange Reality Tastefully

Whether it's a painting, music piece, wedding cake, or a poem, if you put all the pieces together just so, you really can create a work of art. By our choices we all create our life's art. We can focus and finesse our lives just right, and make something very special out of our arrangement. Dip down your bucket and find that source to give you the nourishment and inspiration to arrange your life, so that it gives you the life you deserve. Be the brush and the canvas of your life. Don't hold back, because this it. Be bold. Let it unfold. Go for the gold.

© R. McDougal, 2004

Believing Opens Life's Dream

Life is a "mirror of mind". What you think, is what you get. Know that if something can be done, then it's possible that you can do it. Nothing is accomplished, if nothing is attempted. So be bold and visualize a wonderful life for yourself. You can create, and do create your world. It's been said, "the journey of a thousand miles begins with one step". Why not be bold enough to take that step toward your dream. We're all either winning or learning. Jump into the life's stream and catch your dream.

BELIEVING **O**PENS **L**IFE'S **D**REAM

© R. McDougal, 2004

Bridge Understanding Into Life's Destiny

Understanding gives us the vision to bridge where we're at now, to where we want to be. Step by step, we create where we are, and plant the seeds to where we will be. Understanding gives us the way to find meaning and direction in our lives. Build your life's wonder. Build yourself a world of love and joy. Build a bridge to your dreams. Find out how things work today, so that tomorrow you can sail away.

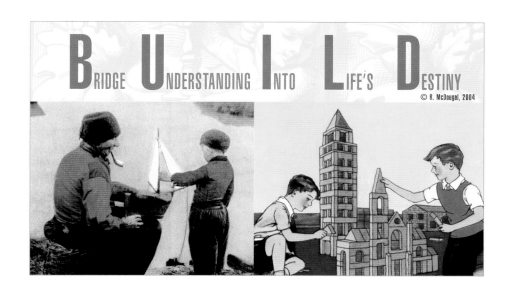

BRIDGE UNDERSTANDING INTO LIFE'S DESTINY

© R. McDougal, 2004

19

Clear Awareness Liberates Magic

Clear awareness is like luminous space. Simple calmness brings clarity. And clarity brings balance and vision. Calm is it's own reward, but it also can give you vision and empowerment to get to where you want to be. Find calm and you will find an unending source of the magic of clarity's vision. When you're calm and clear, your reward is already here. Slow down and find the wonderful vision and magic of a clear mind.

CLEAR **A**WARENESS **L**IBERATES **M**AGIC

© R. McDougal, 2004

Create Answers Now

Yes, you can. "Can't" never could do anything. Bring the elements together, and it can happen. You can create your dreams. Visualize where you want to be, and then start putting the elements together to make it happen. We all have so much potential, when we put our mind to it. One can imagine how, and start to visualize some answers now. Just start, and you will discover which part will complete your life's art. I think I can. I think I can.

© R. McDougal, 2004

Choose Happiness And Reawaken Magic

Implied in this statement, is that we can choose happiness. And it works like a charm. You can learn to appreciate life, instead of constantly judging it, as to how you think it should be. They'll always be good things and bad things in our lives, but we still can find content-ment in accepting this very moment as it is. Good or bad, this moment is perfect-ly "as it is". To accept each moment "as it is", is to give ourselves the charm of contentment's magic and happiness. The choice is yours. It really does work like a charm.

C H A R M

CHOOSE HAPPINESS AND REAWAKEN MAGIC

© R. McDougal, 2004

Daylight Reveals All Men Acting

Everyone is in life's movie. We are all acting out our parts in life's grand pageant. You're the leading actor of your life, so why not make it fun and make it great? We all have good things in our lives, and we all have bad things in our lives. If we can slow the race to a sane pace, then we can connect with the balance and harmony of life. Do the best that you can with what you've got, because we're only on life's stage for a little while. Find a style that lets you smile, mile after mile.

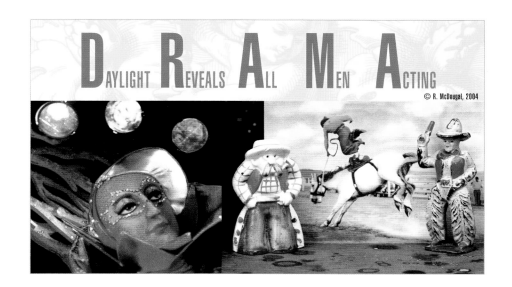

DAYLIGHT **R**EVEALS **A**LL **M**EN **A**CTING

© R. McDougal, 2004

Destiny Reveals Enchantment And Magic

Like a dream, the flame of life is born, then shines brightly, and then fades away. Life can be like a wonderful dream, when we learn to perceive the delicate balance of life and appreciate every passing moment as the gift that it is. Learn to see life in that special way, that honors and reflects the magic and enchantment of our lives. Dream yourself a vision and create a life of wonder and appreciation. "Row, row, row your boat, gently down the stream. Merrily, merrily, merrily, merrily, life is but a dream".

DESTINY **R**EVEALS **E**NCHANTMENT **A**ND **M**AGIC

© R. McDougal, 2004

Finally Let Out Worry

The flow of life is always flowing along. We experience life as a stream of consciousness. If we can find the harmony and stop fighting life so hard, then we can "go with the flow". There is a place of balance and wonder that we can live our lives from. May our lives be an unfolding of discovery and appreciation. May we flow into the harmony and grace of our lives and be carried effortlessly on the river of life. Finally decide to enjoy your ride, and surrender your pride, and put fear aside, and let go. Let worry go, and life will flow.

Finally Love Yourself

If only we can find love. Learn to accept reality and learn to accept yourself. If you are doing the best that you can, then that's all you can ask for. Learn to give love to others, and learn to give it to yourself. We all deserve it, especially ourselves. Love opens you, and love opens others. Open your heart, and you'll find the love that will make your life art. It's so smart. Love is the core that will let you soar. Love is the way to a warm, sunny day. Accept and love yourself today, and you can fly away. Your contentment will lighten your way and brighten your day.

FINALLY **L**OVE **Y**OURSELF

© R. McDougal, 2004

Find Reality Endlessly Entertaining

Isn't life the most wonderful show in town? Before birth we didn't exist. After death we won't be around here. Life is a magic show that is a miraculous gift. Learning to appreciate life leads one to the satisfying wonder and joy of being alive. It's all so amazingly entertaining, when we have the right attitude. And it's all free. So free your imagination to enjoy your life's movie. It's the best show in town. And it's the only show in town. You are free to see and be the eternity of life's wonder and appreciation.

FIND **R**EALITY **E**NDLESSLY **E**NTERTAINING

© R. McDougal, 2004

Give Others Love Daily

Love is what we all want. Realize that everyone and everything is sacred , and deserves honor, respect, and love. We are all part of the miraculous gift of life. Love opens you, and love opens others. To send out love, is to know we are all one and in this together. Be the hero that cares and bares love's gift, and sends others a lift. When you open your heart, you're doing your part. Start things in motion and open your ocean of love. Open your heart and be the one. Someone once said, "Love never costs as much as it pays".

GOLD

GIVE **O**THERS **L**OVE **D**AILY

© R. McDougal, 2004

Help Everyone Awaken Love

To heal is to become whole and be in harmony. To let go of disease (dis-ease), is to be in the flow of the nourishing life force. To reach out and love, is to help heal ourselves and others. Let love show us a way to reflect our respect. To heal is the deal. Be a light so that others might see. Open your heart and show others the art of how to be. Let love guide your way to a brand new day. You can reflect the warm, loving feeling of healing.

HEAL

HELP EVERYONE AWAKEN LOVE

© R. McDougal, 2004

Help Everyone Awaken Real Trust

The greatest thing you can do for anyone is to make them feel like they're okay. Open your heart, and respect and support your fellow man and woman who, like yourself, are trying the best they know how to carry their heavy load. The gift of acceptance is the ultimate gift to another. Give a little understanding. Give a little lift. Give a little heart. Open your heart and do your part. Open hearts open magic.

H E A R T

Help Everyone Awaken Real Trust

© R. McDougal, 2004

Happy Endings Really Occur

Life can be great, and is great, when we learn to see it in that special way. Everyone wants to know that "happy endings really occur". We don't live in the past or the future, so make your happy endings and happy beginnings happen today, since today is all that we have. Happiness is here for the taking. Create your happiness today, and you can sail away. Being a hero or being happy is a choice. Life is just as wonderful as you think it is. So, think it is.

HERO
Happy Endings Really Occur

© R. McDougal, 2004

Heal Our Mother Earth

We are in big trouble, if we don't stop over-developing and over-populating of our planet. You don't have to be a rocket-scientist to know that the earth's well-being has been sacrificed for short-term profits. More and more people are fighting for less and less dwindling resources. Let's all stand up and be responsible for getting our environment healthy and in balance. This is the only planet we have. We are playing Russian Roulette with our survival. We all deserve better. Do your part to make a new start.

Imagination Develops Easy Answers

Go fishing with that wonderful imagination of yours. It's amazing what you can find, when you really explore the possibilities. Discover something new. Discover something just for you.

There are so many answers just waiting to be uncovered. The idea is to use your imagination to discover new ways of seeing and new ways of being. Just imagine!

© R. McDougal, 2004

Just Orchestrating Balance

Our ongoing job in life is to find a balance with all the needs and challenges we have coming towards us. Life is a dance, and we have to juggle things to find our sense of balance. May we find that center, that gives us the balance to find the grace and magic of life. Let go of attachments and judgments, and let your mind be in harmony. It's a dance. It's a trance. It's a romance with the balance of life.

JUST **O**RCHESTRATING **B**ALANCE

© R. McDougal, 2004

Just Open Yourself

Only when we open to the wonder of life will we experience the joy we deserve. Each one of us is the only one who can do it for ourselves. Opening is freeing. Opening is being. Opening is trusting. Go ahead and open to the joy that is your birthright. You have everything to gain and nothing to lose. Why not shed any dread, and be happy instead? Nobody can see inside your head. The choice is yours. Just open yourself.

JOY

JUST OPEN YOURSELF

© R. McDougal, 2004

Keep Empowering Yourself

One of the keys to life is to use your attention to focus on what you want to create. Where you put your attention, energy will follow. Life is a mirror of mind. What you think is what you get. Tap into the flow of life and watch things happen. Just let go and start to flow, and soon you'll know. It's been said, "The journey of 10,000 miles begins beneath your feet". The key is let yourself free your own energy with the focus of your vision. Unlock the power of your own mind, and you'll be amazed at what you can find. The key is to let awareness keep empowering your life.

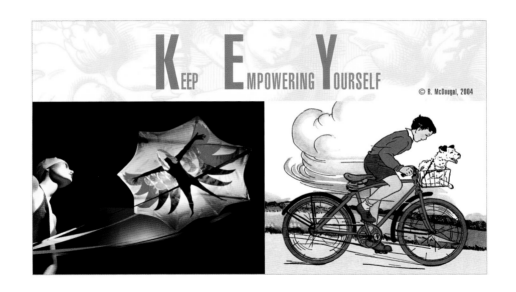

KEEP EMPOWERING YOURSELF

© R. McDougal, 2004

Let It Flow Effortlessly

The gift of life is a wonderful thing. Often we get so caught up in the rush of things, that we get full of tension. When we aren't paying attention, we identify with the thoughts and emotions and take everything personally. We all have problems, but it's our attitude that determines the quality of our lives.

Stress never helped anyone. Just relax into knowing that you are doing the best you can. Be content in knowing that at this moment, this is the way it is, no more and no less. Just go with the flow. Row, row, row your boat, gently down the stream. When you flow effortlessly, life is but a dream.

LIFE

Let It Gently Happen Today

Just let it happen. Life flows on it's own. You don't have to push the river. When you go with the flow, life will gently carry you. The light of mind gives you the presence to receive life's presents. Stop the hurry. Stop the worry. Let go of stress, or you'll be a mess. Tread lightly. Loosen up. Let your light shine. This life can really be quite fine. Just let it gently happen today. Let the light of your mind brighten your day.

LIGHT

Let It Gently Happen Today

© R. McDougal, 2004

Let Inner Vision Empower

The vision of the sage reminds us, "what you think, is what you get". Your inner vision defines your world. You can learn to see the world where you are always a winner, no matter what happens. Nothing can harm your mind, because your mind is nothing. It is no thing. When you don't make your happiness dependent on something outside yourself, you empower yourself with contentment. Give yourself the vision to let your mind find life's wonder. Just be. Just see. Just free that vision that enchants your life. Just live and let live.

L I V E

Let Inner Vision Empower

© R. McDougal, 2004

Let Others' Visions Exist

One of the greatest gifts we can give people is to let them have their own vision. Appreciate that everyone has their own unique way of seeing things. Allow them to have their own picture of the world. Love is letting go of thinking your way is better for everyone. Love is honoring and respecting others, as you would like to be. Just like you have your certain way, others do too. Love lets others be who they are. As long as someone is not stepping on anyone's toes, we should let them be free to see as they want to be.

LOVE

LET **O**THERS' **V**ISIONS **E**XIST

© R. McDougal, 2004

Listen Until Clarity Illuminates Destiny

When we have clarity, we can see clearly. It pays big dividends to slow down and gather ourselves. When we are quiet, we become centered and in balance. With silence, clarity will arise and shed light on our situation, as well as, the big picture. If you let it flower, it will give your vision power. Listen until it starts to glisten. Let it flow until you know. When you let it be, you start to see.

Mind's Awareness Generates Infinite Creation

Everything exists in your mind. It sounds crazy, but when you think about it, you realize that, literally, the totality of your experience takes place in your awareness. If something doesn't exist in your awareness, it doesn't exist for you. Life is a flow of awareness, arising and then falling away. What you are looking for, is what is looking. The infinite universe all comes out of your mind. All of creation is experienced in your awareness, and nowhere else. So enjoy and appreciate your stream of consciousness, because it is that magic stage where we live our lives.

MAGIC

MIND'S **A**WARENESS **G**ENERATES **I**NFINITE **C**REATION

© R. McDougal, 2004

Mirroring Eternity

Your mind mirrors the infinite universe. You are it, and it is you. Really there is no permanent "me", "I", or "self". These are concepts that are reference points for the ever-changing and evolving mind-body process. But the luminous light of mind mirrors life's miraculous show. If you take away the world, the mind disappears. And if you take away the mind, the world disappears. We mirror life and life mirrors us. When we are selfless, we become one with it all. May you finally realize that the mind mirrors the oneness and eternity of our life's awareness.

MIRRORING ETERNITY

© R. McDougal, 2004

Magically Expand The Edge Of Reality

With your mind's light, you can light up the night. With your will power and focus, you can create your dreams. As you evolve and learn more about life, your world of possibilities truly expands. The more you know, the more you grow. The world is just what you think it is. So learn to see a growing world of wonderful possibilities. Let your inner light guide your way and expand your horizons. Let it flow and let it grow into life's wonderful show. Les Brown said, "Shoot for the moon. Even if you miss, you will land among the stars."

METEOR

MAGICALLY EXPAND THE EDGE OF REALITY

© R. McDougal, 2004

Mind Is Reality And Creates Life's Existence

Your whole life is in your mind. It's a miracle. We think, we are here, and the "world" is out there. But the "world out there" is an idea and experience that takes place in our mind, in our awareness. Take away your mind, and the world disappears. Take away the world, and your mind disappears. Your mind is the fundamental reality, since that is the place where you experience everything. When you change your perception of the world, the world literally changes for you. So appreciate life's dance, get out of your trance, and enjoy the wonderful expanse of the miracle of life.

Making Yourself Selfless Touches Infinity's Core

"As long as there is one to suffer, he or she will." The idea of a "me", "I", or "ego", is merely that, an idea, a reference point. "Me" is an idea that refers to our ongoing mind-body process, which is ever changing. But you don't have to take everything personally. You can identify with life's greater whole, and stop seeing things as "me" against the world. Your mind is not divided unless you create the division. It's just One Mind's cosmic dance. Relax. Nothing can harm your mind, because your mind is nothing (no-thing). It's just the spacious stage, where we enjoy our life's movie. It's a wonderful and mystical thing.

MYSTIC

Making Yourself Selfless Touches Infinity's Core

© R. McDougal, 2004

Make Yourself The Hero

Everyone admires the hero. Somebody has to step up and be the hero. You can be a hero. The ball's in your court. If you know how lucky you feel when someone helps you, when you're in need, then you can be the "hero" that reaches out and helps someone else. To give is to live. It's so right to help, since this is your world. And when we focus on being a team player, we minimize thinking about our own problems. Carry the hero's light that shines so bright. Someone has to care. Someone has to share. Start here. Start now. You already know how.

© R. McDougal, 2004

Only Now Exists

We hear the idea of "one world", "one planet", "one people", and "one mind". Taking in everything, we have "one" big experience, the universe, which means "one-verse". "Here" is the center of space. And "now" is the center of time. The time is always now. The words "past" and "future" are concepts that are experienced only in the present. It's great to have memories and to have dreams, but appreciate and realize that you only live right now. Ultimately, right now is the only game in town. So find your place and find your grace, in the magic space of the ever-present moment of now. It's the one.

ONLY NOW EXISTS

© R. McDougal, 2004

Put Awareness To Heart

You can arrive at that hero's view and bring heart to your life's path. Combining awareness and caring, we can evolve to that place of knowing and helping to create a better world. To the person of knowledge, every step of our life's path is as important as the journey's end. We can only pick the fruit of life in this present moment. May the road of life inspire you to open your heart and carry your load with graceful appreciation and dignity. May your heart's guiding light illuminate the path for you and all to see.

Project Life's Answers Now

If we don't know where we're going, then any road will do. But if we actually want to accomplish something and get somewhere, then first we must visualize it. Visualize where you want to be, and then work backwards and figure out each step to get you there. It's called a "plan". Make a plan and know you can. Start things in motion. Take it and bake it, even fake it, and it can start to happen. The world is your oyster, if you know how to open it. The world is a wonderful treasure, and you can create the key with your vision. Focus on how now.

Ride Evolution And Learn

Let us ride evolution and learn life's mysteries. When we surrender to the moment and go with the flow, we can learn how to ride life's waves, and discover its show. We ride life's ever-changing flow into this endless moment. We realize that even though life's movie is continuously changing, in our mind, we can stay calm and content and balanced in the center of the parade of life. May we continue to learn with every turn. May we get real and learn how to deal with the magically unfolding ride of our lives. This is your hour. Flower into your power. Find the glide in your ride.

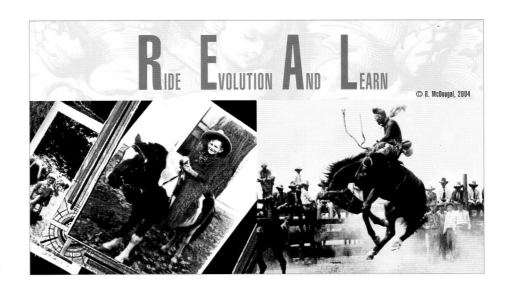

R E A L

RIDE EVOLUTION AND LEARN

© R. McDougal, 2004

Reawaken Into Creation's Happiness

We're are all so very rich, if we only knew it. The incredible gift of life and all of its phenomenal rewards are infinitely rich and wonderful. The joy of appreciating life can be your greatest treasure. Be fulfilled in knowing that life is a vast resource of endless inspiration and discovery. The endless flower of now continually offers up it's rich rewards. Take time for today, since this life is always slipping away. So take time to savor and appreciate the miracle life's many riches. Slow down and remember and reawaken into creation's happiness. When you get really clear, you can see that the vast riches of your life are already here.

RICH

Reawaken Into Creation's Happiness

© R. McDougal, 2004

Realize Imagination Possesses Eternity

We are all so ripe with the possibility. With our imagination and our intuition, we can realize our dreams. Anything we can imagine, our awareness breathes life into. Eternity is here and now forever. The essence of your mind, which is no-thing, is beyond birth or death. It's that "is-ness" quality of your mind. We can experience the infinite in the finite, when we let ourselves become it. Life is a "Mirror of Mind". What you think, is what you get. What you don't think, is the infinite. May you realize and taste the wonderful, infinite, eternal fruit that is your own mind.

Reach Out – Awaken Dreams

We're all on our journey on the road of life. Life is an ongoing dialectic, we create it, and it creates us. It's okay to reach out and go for it, because nothing can harm your mind, because your mind is nothing (no-thing). With some vision and some heart, some knowledge and experience, we can reawaken a wonderful life. When you get really clear, you can realize that your dreams are already here. You truly can awaken your dreams. Just open the door. There's so much in store, when you realize that you're already on the distant shore. Your dreams are right here waiting for you to awaken to them.

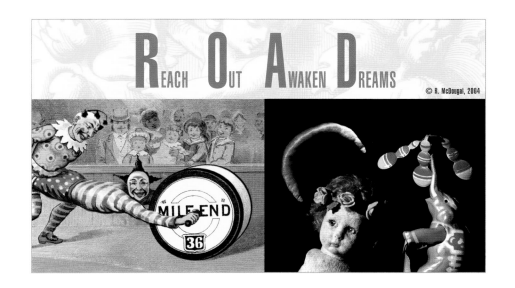

Slowing Allows Fast Evolution

Mahatma Gandhi said, "There is more to life than increasing its speed." Sometimes we get going so fast, that we lose our place. We lose perspective of who we are and where we're going. Stress is a disease (dis-ease). Ironically, if we slow down and gather ourselves, we can soon remember that place inside where things are clear and peaceful and in harmony. We can remember how to find the balance of our lives and appreciate the miracle of life. Slow down and see. Slow down and be. Slow down and free that safe place of grace, where we feel right at home right now.

Skip Asking — Give Endlessly

Everyone has a burden to carry through life, just as we do. When we experience life's suffering, it gives us the insight to relate to others' pain. When someone helps us, we know how much it means to us. Generosity lifts us, as it lifts others. The sage and the hero have always been revered and appreciated in all cultures, because of their wisdom, compassion and willingness to help others. So find that generous shift, and give someone a lift. It's the ultimate gift. The wise ones know how to open their heart and practice the hero art. Why not start? The more you give, the more you live.

SKIP **A**SKING **G**IVE **E**NDLESSLY

© R. McDougal, 2004

Simply Awaken Into Life

Get off the sidelines and jump into the magic of your own life. Reawaken into the magic of seeing and the flow of being, and let it carry you down the river of life. Acceptance, appreciation, and awareness let you flow with joy and go with grace. Put up your sail and glide through the unfolding of your life's stream. Sail into now. You've always known how. Every shift is a brand new gift. May the winds of life sail you to that happy place, where you can stop the endless chase, and live in grace. May you discover how to find the paradise in right now.

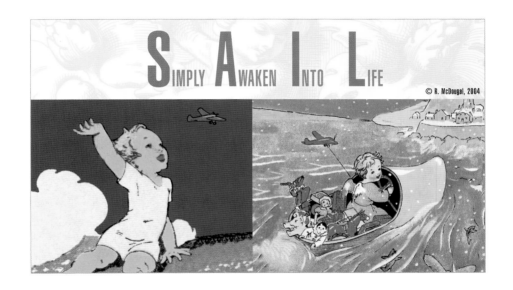

Simply Open And Receive

To receive anything in life, we must be open to it. So many people close themselves off and aren't open to the wonderful gifts of life. We have to learn that it's okay to open, because nothing can harm your mind. Nobody can ever get inside your head and make you uptight or afraid. The thoughts and emotions are just figs and twigs and jigs floating on the river of life. Don't worry about anything. It's all a passing show. Open to the light, and you will be alright. Then you can become the delight of the day and the night. Give yourself flight. Open your door and let yourself soar.

© R. McDougal, 2004

Simply Trust Your Life's Essence

To find that style that will make you smile, just be yourself. If you just be yourself, you can't lose. And if you try to be something you're not, you can't win. Just do the best you can with what you've got and be content. Nobody can ask you to do more than that. We're all in the parade of life, that miracle we are all witness to. At each moment everyone is acting out his or her part in life's dance. Be the style that will let you smile, mile after mile, through trial after trial. Trust is a must. Trust opens the door to let your mind soar. Just think you're okay, then you'll think you're okay. Life is a Mirror of Mind.

STYLE

SIMPLY **T**RUST **Y**OUR **L**IFE'S **E**SSENCE

© R. McDougal, 2004

Trust Indestructible Mind's Eternity

The ultimate trust is born in knowing that nothing can harm your mind, because your mind is nothing. It's just the context where things happen. Some call the mind the "diamond" or the "jewel", because it is indestructible, obviously, because nothing can harm nothing. Again, since mind is everything, yet nothing at all, it is likened to infinity and eternity. The mystery of your mind is truly impossible to define. It's time to appreciate the wonderful miracle of your own mind. Go for a ride inside and discover the infinite universe is in your own mind. It's time to find the infinite joy of your own mind.

TIME

TRUST **I**NDESTRUCTIBLE **M**IND'S **E**TERNITY

© R. McDougal, 2004

Take Responsibility Yourself

Woody Allen once said, "Eighty percent of success is just showing up." There are so many people that don't even try. It's really not that hard, if you just put one foot in front of the other and fall forward. Lao Tzu said, "The journey a thousand miles begins with one step." If you put the ingredients together, things will happen. Most people have similar potential, but some succeed because they are willing to focus and use will-power to make things happen. Nothing ventured, nothing gained. So as you sow, so shall you reap. Just go for it. Just try. We're all always either winning or learning.

Vision Illuminates Enchantment's Wonder

Your world is created by your point of view. What you think is what you get. Hocus-pocus, it's all how you focus. Your point of view defines what's there for you. An enchanting wonderland is waiting for you in your imagination. An infinite world of possibility is yours to explore. So take time to unwind and find the riches in your own mind. Find a fabulous view that's just right for you. Reawaken into your own wonderland, where it feels really grand. Seeing is freeing. Discover the view that's enchanted for you.

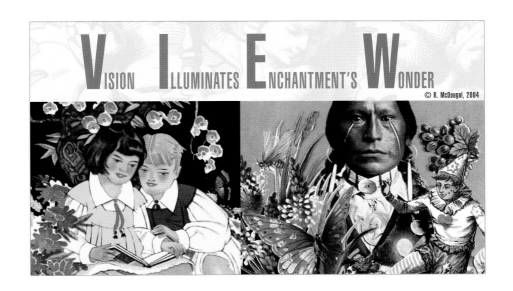

Waken Into Timeless Happiness Inside Now

You can search for happiness the world over, but you will never find it anywhere, except within yourself. Happiness comes from inner contentment brought about by creating balance and harmony in our lives. We can learn to accept this moment for what it is, and appreciate that for now things are perfectly as they are. The trick is to stop constantly judging life against our yardstick of how we think it should be. Just learn to slow, and let go, and your happiness will start to show. Take a ride inside. You will finally win, and realize your happiness has always been right within.

WAKEN **I**NTO **T**IMELESS **H**APPINESS **I**NSIDE **N**OW

© R. McDougal, 2004

Wonder's Openness Reawakens Life's Dance

Your world is the miracle of life. This is our moment to be on stage and do our dance of life. This life is mostly what you choose to create, and how you choose to perceive the world. Like a mirror, your mind reflects the meanings you project. So let life's dance and song carry you along in the kaleidoscope of time. The world is a wonderful dance, when we find our stance. It's a dance. It's a trance. It's a prance. It's a romance with life's wonder. So let the world be your stage where you can freely engage with your ongoing sage. You have come of age. Let go and simply flow into the magic of your life's dance.

WORLD

WONDER'S **O**PENNESS **R**EAWAKENS **L**IFE'S **D**ANCE

© R. McDougal, 2004

You Empower Solutions

Yes, you can! So many people are looking for someone else to do something, or hope things will change by themselves. If you just look inside, you will discover so many possibilities. Use your imagination and think of how things might be, and what it takes to make it happen. Just the act of exploring will lead to answers. You have so many answers inside, just waiting to be discovered. Put on your inner glasses and give it a good look. I think I can. I think I can. I know you can. Yes, you can empower yourself. And it feels so good. Yes, you can. Yes, you can.

Acknowledgements

I would like to acknowledge my father and mother's support and unconditional love. The acronyms are my way of returning their generosity and sharing with all the fruits of my insights & reflections that have come my way.

My two sons, Austin and Connor, are the joy of my life. Their enthusiasm and fresh observations are wonderful insights from the next generation.

I want to thank Lynne McDougal for her great character and generosity.

Thanks also to: Barry Zaid, Chris Knight, David Bush, Andrew Webb, Richard Aram, Denny and Tom Fernandez, Deke McClelland, Dennis Mayer, Bonnie & George Loizos, Jose Arguelles, Jerry Hodges, Lynn Milot, Taulere and Arrone Appel, Cha Cha and Leslie, Merry Witty, Jack Rudd, Jeff Markel, Steve James, Barbee James, Jillian Klarl, Tony and Kersti, Sherry Hart, Mark and Joan Kraus and Carolyn Gianotti, Karen Kreutzer, Ted Ringer, Wylie and Margaret Johnson. A heartful thanks to Kalu Rinpoche and the Dalai Lama. And a special thanks to John Rainey for his brilliant design and generous heart.